"BRING THE CLASSICS TO LIFE"

LITTLE WOMEN

Level 1

Series Designer
Philip J. Solimene

Editor
Laura M. Toles

EDCON

Story Adaptor
Jacqueline Nightingale

Author
Louisa May Alcott

About the Author

Louisa May Alcott was born in Germantown, Pennsylvania on November 29, 1832. She was the second oldest of four sisters. She received most of her early schooling from her father as he was a teacher. Her story "Little Women" is about many of her own true experiences. Hard times fell upon her family, and Louisa worked many jobs to help her parents. She was a seamstress, a nurse, and a school teacher, just to name a few. She started to write in hopes of making more money. "Little Women" is her most well-known book. On March 6, 1888, only days after her father had passed away, Louisa May Alcott died.

Copyright © 1992
A/V Concepts Corp.
Long Island, New York

Printed in U.S.A.
ISBN# 1-55576-047-3

CONTENTS

WORDS USED

Story 21	Story 22	Story 23	Story 24	Story 25
KEY WORDS				
breakfast	dress	aunt	building	beautiful
hair	grandfather	fire	secret	cry
money	party	job	story	long
next	thank	sisters	their	mail
pretty	window	write	time	well

NECESSARY WORDS				
Army		after	fall	barber
Christmas		angry	newspaper	
		found		
		lazy		

WORDS USED

Story 26	Story 27	Story 28	Story 29	Story 30
KEY WORDS				
become	children	another	anyone	grandmother
everyone	good-by	right	birthday	important
surprise	great	shining	coming	small
twins	met	talk	hard	smart
women	school	without	sitting	such

Story 26	Story 27	Story 28	Story 29	Story 30
NECESSARY WORDS				
college	family	hotel	knock	arms
marry	meet	life	those	became
own		nothing	umbrella	picked
take				rest
wedding				
will				

CHRISTMAS AT THE MARCH HOUSE

PREPARATION

Key Words

breakfast	(brek′ fast)	1. the first meal of the day 2. eat breakfast *I cannot start my day without <u>breakfast</u>.*
hair	(hãr)	1. fine thread-like growth from the skin 2. mass of such growths *My <u>hair</u> got wet when I went into the water.*
money	(mun′ē)	1. coins of gold, silver or paper notes issued by the government 2. wealth *The man made his <u>money</u> by working very hard.*
next	(nekst)	1. nearest 2. having nothing of the same kind coming in between *I was <u>next</u> on line in the store.*
pretty	(prit′ē)	pleasing *The boy smiled at the <u>pretty</u> girl in the park.*

CHRISTMAS AT THE MARCH HOUSE

Necessary Words

Army ('är-mē) a large group of men and women trained for war
All the men and women left to go into the Army.

Christmas ('Kris-məs) a holiday on December 25 when people give gifts and have a merry time
I like to be with my whole family on Christmas Day.

People

Amy The youngest and prettiest of the March girls (about 12 years old).

Beth The shyest and kindest of the March girls (13 years old).

Jo The tomboy of the girls. She wished to be a famous writer (15 years old).

Meg The oldest of the March sisters (16 years old).

Mr. March Loving father of the March girls. He was called into the Army.

Mrs. March Mother of the March girls. She is a kind, loving, caring person.

CHRISTMAS AT THE MARCH HOUSE

Each of the girls plan to buy something for their mother with the money they have.

Preview:
1. Read the name of the story.
2. Look at the picture.
3. Read the sentence under the picture.
4. Read the first three paragraphs of the story.
5. Then answer the following question.

You learned from your preview that the girls had
_____ a. lots of money.
_____ b. very little money.
_____ c. no mother or father.
_____ d. no shoes.

Turn to the Comprehension Check on page 10 for the right answer.

Now read the story.

Read to find out what the March family does on Christmas Day.

CHRISTMAS AT THE MARCH HOUSE

"Christmas will not be fun if we don't get new things," said Jo March.

"Why can't we have money like other people?" said Meg. She looked down at her old shoes.

"Other girls have lots of nice things. We have very little," said Amy.

"We have Father and Mother. And we have enough to get by," said Beth.

"But Father is not here!" said Jo. "He could be away for a year or more." Mr. March was away helping the Army.

The four March girls were getting ready for Christmas. They did not have a lot of money. They did have lots of love.

Meg was the oldest. She was pretty with big eyes and soft, red hair. Then there was Jo. She had dark brown hair. Jo liked to make up plays. The girls would act them out. She wished she were a boy, and acted like one.

Next came Beth. She had the kindest face. She was always good.

Last of the March girls, was Amy. She was as pretty as a picture and thought so, too.

The girls heard a noise from outside. Mother was home at last. She had gone to help a woman who could not get up and around. The woman had no food to eat.

Mother thought it would be nice to bring Christmas breakfast to the woman. The girls said they would be happy to. That morning, they packed a box of food to take to her.

When Mrs. March and the girls got home, a big breakfast had been cooked for them. It was from the old man who lived in the house next door. The food was so good.

Mother said she had more good news. It was a letter from Father. The girls listened as she read to them. Father was doing fine. He missed them and loved them.

The rest of the day the March girls acted out one of Jo's plays. They laughed and had a fun day.

Mother said it was the best Christmas they had in years.

CHRISTMAS AT THE MARCH HOUSE

COMPREHENSION CHECK

> **Preview Answer:**
>
> b.   very little money.

Choose the best answer.

1. Mr. March, the girls' father, is
   _____ a.   not living.
   _____ b.   at work.
   _____ c.   away helping the Army.
   _____ d.   very mean.

2. The four March girls did not have a lot of money, but they did have lots of
   _____ a.   clothes.
   _____ b.   food.
   _____ c.   hate.
   _____ d.   love.

3. Who is the oldest of the March girls?
   _____ a.   Meg
   _____ b.   Jo
   _____ c.   Beth
   _____ d.   Amy

4. Which of the sisters wishes she was a boy?
   _____ a.   Meg
   _____ b.   Jo
   _____ c.   Beth
   _____ d.   Amy

5. In this story, Mrs. March had gone to
   _____ a.   the zoo.
   _____ b.   the store.
   _____ c.   the Army to be with Mr. March.
   _____ d.   help a woman who could not get out of bed.

6. Mrs. March and the girls thought it would be nice to
   _____ a.   give the woman a Christmas breakfast.
   _____ b.   paint the house.
   _____ c.   have a big party.
   _____ d.   take a walk down to the bridge.

7. When the Marches got home, waiting for them was
   _____ a.   their father.
   _____ b.   the man next door.
   _____ c.   a big breakfast.
   _____ d.   danger.

8. Why do you think the man next door sent breakfast to the Marches on Christmas Day?
   _____ a.   He found out about the kind thing they had done.
   _____ b.   He was in love with them.
   _____ c.   Mr. March told him they had no food.
   _____ d.   They asked him to.

9. Another name for this story could be
   _____ a.   "A Very Sad Day."
   _____ b.   "Off to the Army."
   _____ c.   "Pretty as a Picture."
   _____ d.   "Five Kind People."

10. This story is mainly about
    _____ a.   the kind March family.
    _____ b.   the mean March family.
    _____ c.   the lost March family.
    _____ d.   a sad Christmas Day.

Check your answers with the key on page 67.

This page may be reproduced for classroom use.

CHRISTMAS AT THE MARCH HOUSE

VOCABULARY CHECK

breakfast	hair	money	next	pretty

I. Sentences to Finish

Fill in the blank in each sentence with the correct key word from the box above.

1. Please come here and sit _____ to me.

2. I used to have long _____ until I cut it off.

3. My new hat is very _____ .

4. You should begin your day with a good _____ .

5. I could not buy anything because I left my _____ home.

II. Crossword Puzzle

Use the words from the box above to fill in the puzzle. Use the meanings below to help you choose the right answer.

Across

1. first meal of the day

3. coins

Down

2. thread-like growth from the skin

4. pleasing

5. nearest

Check your answers with the key on page 69.

This page may be reproduced for classroom use.

THE BOY NEXT DOOR

PREPARATION

Key Words

dress   (dres)
1. the usual outer garment worn by women, girls and babies
2. clothing, especially outer clothing
3. put clothes on
I wore a red dress to the party.

grandfather   (grand′ fä THər)
1. father of one's father or mother
2. any forefather
My grandfather and I go fishing in the summer.

party   (par′ tē)
group of people doing something together
A surprise birthday party has been planned for my friend.

thank   (thangk)
1. say "thank you" when someone does something nice
I said thank you to the girl for helping me get up.

window   (win′ dō)
1. an opening in a wall or roof to let light or air in
2. such an opening with its frame and glass
The children looked out the window and watched the snow come down.

THE BOY NEXT DOOR

People

Laurie Laurence   the boy who lives next door to the March home (about 16 years old)

Mr. Laurence   Grandfather of Laurie Laurence; he is a kind old man with much money who lives in a grand house.

THE BOY NEXT DOOR

Jo could be very happy in a big room such as this, with many books and pictures.

Preview:　　1.　Read the name of the story.
　　　　　　　2.　Look at the picture.
　　　　　　　3.　Read the sentence under the picture.
　　　　　　　4.　Read the first two paragraphs of the story.
　　　　　　　5.　Then answer the following question.

You learned from your preview that

_____ a.　the girls had a party.
_____ b.　the girls found a pot of gold.
_____ c.　Laurie Laurence ran away from home.
_____ d.　Laurie Laurence lives next door to the Marches.

Turn to the Comprehension Check on page 16 for the right answer.

Now read the story.

Read to find out about Jo's day at the Laurence house.

THE BOY NEXT DOOR

The March girls went to a New Year's party. Meg had on a blue dress. Jo looked pretty in red. Beth had on green, and Amy looked grand in her gold dress.

At the party, Jo talked to Laurie Laurence most of the night. Laurie lived in the house next to them with his grandfather, Mr. Laurence. They had lots of money.

Days later, Jo was out walking. She stopped outside the Laurence home. Laurie was looking out his window. He opened the window and called to Jo. He said to come in. Mrs. March said she could go to see Laurie.

Jo ran to the house. She had never been in a house this big or grand. A man with a stone face showed Jo into the living room where Laurie was sitting. It was a big room with many fine things around. There were many books and pictures to look at.

Jo looked at a picture of Mr. Laurence. She thought she could be afraid of him. Jo heard a noise in the room. When she looked around, she was face-to-face with Mr. Laurence. Seeing his soft eyes and kind face, Jo was not afraid of him.

Now Jo could thank Mr. Laurence for giving them breakfast on Christmas morning. Jo got a "thank you" from Mr. Laurence for coming to see Laurie. Not too many people came to see them.

Mr. Laurence said Mother and the girls could come over any day they wished. He would be glad to see them.

The cook made a nice lunch for Jo, Laurie and his grandfather. When lunch was over, Jo ran home.

Jo called to Mother and the girls to sit by her. They listened as Jo told them of her day in the Laurence home. Jo said Mr. Laurence was a fine old man and very nice.

From that day on, the Marches and the Laurences were good friends.

THE BOY NEXT DOOR

COMPREHENSION CHECK

Choose the best answer.

1. At the New Year's party, who did Jo talk with most of the night?
   _____ a.   Laurie Laurence
   _____ b.   Meg March
   _____ c.   Amy March
   _____ d.   Beth March

2. The Laurence family had
   _____ a.   eight children.
   _____ b.   a small house.
   _____ c.   many dogs and cats.
   _____ d.   lots of money.

3. Jo was happy to go to Laurie's house because
   _____ a.   she was going to babysit.
   _____ b.   she had never been in a house so big and grand.
   _____ c.   she wanted to get away from her home.
   _____ d.   the Laurences were having a party.

4. When Jo came face-to-face with Mr. Laurence,
   _____ a.   she ran and hid.
   _____ b.   she started to cry.
   _____ c.   she was no longer afraid of him.
   _____ d.   she knew she hated him even more than ever.

5. Mr. Laurence thanked Jo for
   _____ a.   the party.
   _____ b.   going home early.
   _____ c.   giving him breakfast on Christmas morning.
   _____ d.   coming to see Laurie.

6. Laurie was happy that Jo came to see him because
   _____ a.   he didn't have many friends.
   _____ b.   she was pretty.
   _____ c.   she helped him plan his party.
   _____ d.   she gave back dishes from breakfast.

7. Mr. Laurence told Jo
   _____ a.   never to come back.
   _____ b.   that her mother and sisters could come over any day.
   _____ c.   to leave Laurie alone.
   _____ d.   that she had to pay him for her lunch.

8. From that day on,
   _____ a.   the Marches and the Laurences were good friends.
   _____ b.   Jo never spoke to Laurie again.
   _____ c.   Jo never spoke to Laurie's grandfather again.
   _____ d.   Jo lived with the Laurence family.

9. Another name for this story could be
   _____ a.   "Running Away From Home."
   _____ b.   "Why Me?"
   _____ c.   "A Day at the Laurence House."
   _____ d.   "No More Fighting."

10. This story is mainly about
   _____ a.   Jo leaving home.
   _____ b.   Jo making friends with the people next door.
   _____ c.   Laurie running away.
   _____ d.   Jo and Laurie fighting.

Check your answers with the key on page 67.

This page may be reproduced for classroom use.

THE BOY NEXT DOOR

VOCABULARY CHECK

dress	grandfather	party	thank	window

I. Sentences to Finish

Fill in the blank in each sentence with the correct key word from the box above.

1. My _____ is coming over to stay with us.

2. Mother went to the store to buy a cake for the _____ .

3. I can't wait to wear my new _____ .

4. "Who broke the _____ ?" asked the teacher.

5. I want to _____ all my friends for coming to help me.

II. Word Use

Put a check next to YES if the sentence makes sense. Put a check next to NO if the sentence does not make sense.

1. My friends and I are going to a <u>party</u>.   _____ Yes _____ No

2. It was too cold out to wear a <u>dress</u>.   _____ Yes _____ No

3. My mother's brother is my <u>grandfather</u>.   _____ Yes _____ No

4. Always put milk in the <u>window</u> to keep it cold.   _____ Yes _____ No

5. I want to <u>thank</u> you for being so kind.   _____ Yes _____ No

Check your answers with the key on page 69.

SUNNY DAYS OF SPRING

PREPARATION

Key Words

aunt ('ant)
1. a sister of one's father or mother
2. the wife of one's uncle
   My aunt and I went shopping for a new dress.

fire ('fīr)
1. the light and heat and especially the flame produced by burning
2. something burning
3. warmth
   We all sat near the fire to get warm.

job ('jäb)
1. a piece of work, especially for a fixed price for the whole task
2. a duty
3. work; employment
   It was my job to keep the kitchen clean.

sisters ('sis - tər)
1. a girl or woman related to a person by having the same mother and father
2. one of the same kind regarded as nearly related
   I have two sisters, and we all get along well.

write (rīt)
writing (rīt ing)
1. to form letters or words with pen or pencil
2. to put words on paper
3. to make up and set down words for others to read as a story or book
   I like to write short stories; writing books takes too long.

SUNNY DAYS OF SPRING

Necessary Words

after   (af′ tər)   later in time than; following
>*It was my turn, after Betty.*

angry   (ang′ grē)   showing or having the feeling one has toward someone or something that hurts, annoys, etc.
>*I was angry because they were calling me names.*

found   (found)   past tense of find
>*I found my hat in the car.*

lazy   (lā′ zē)   not willing to work or be active; moving slowly
>*I feel lazy today; I don't want to do anything.*

People

Aunt March   an old aunt on the March side of the family, who had a lot of money

John Brooke   Laurie's teacher

teacher   person who teaches

Places

theater   (thē′ ə ter)   a place where plays are acted or motion pictures are shown

SUNNY DAYS OF SPRING

Jo let Laurie win this time because he had been so nice to Beth. Laurie went to see the Marches often.

Preview:
1. Read the name of the story.
2. Look at the picture.
3. Read the sentences under the picture.
4. Read the first two paragraphs of the story.
5. Then answer the following question.

You learned from your preview that the Laurences and the Marches
_____ a. became good friends.
_____ b. never spoke to one another again.
_____ c. hated each other.
_____ d. had a big fight.

Turn to the Comprehension Check on page 22 for the right answer.

Now read the story.

Read to find out more about the March sisters.

SUNNY DAYS OF SPRING

The cold days after New Year's went by fast. By now the Marches and the Laurences were good friends. The sunny days of spring had come at last.

Meg got a job looking after three sisters and two brothers. On one of these fine days, Meg got to be friends with John Brooke. He was Laurie's teacher.

Jo got a little money to stay with old Aunt March. Aunt March had lots of money. Jo read to her in the morning. Then Aunt March would rest. Jo would read her aunt's books and write plays.

Beth was happy to stay home and help Mother. Amy, on the other hand, was lazy. She felt it was her job to do good in her book work. She would sit around and make pretty pictures most of the day.

There are days when the most loving of sisters do not get along. The March sisters had them, too.

One fine day, Jo, Meg, and Laurie were going out to the theater. Amy wished she could go with them. Jo said no. Amy got angry with her. After they left, Amy took Jo's writing book. She placed it in the fire. When Jo found out, she said she would never forget what Amy did to her.

Some days later, Jo and Laurie walked to the lake. Jo knew that Amy was not far from them, but she acted like she didn't see her. Amy fell into the water. Seeing her in danger, Laurie jumped in. He helped Amy out. A wet, cold Amy went home to sit by the fire.

When Jo got home, she was sorry for being angry at Amy and leaving her home. She said Amy could go along with her and Laurie from then on.

Jo and Amy were loving sisters and friends again.

SUNNY DAYS OF SPRING

COMPREHENSION CHECK

Choose the best answer.

1. Meg had a job
   _____ a. in a school.
   _____ b. in the food store.
   _____ c. reading to Aunt March.
   _____ d. looking after five children.

2. Jo had a job
   _____ a. taking care of Aunt March.
   _____ b. baby-sitting five children.
   _____ c. cooking for some people.
   _____ d. teaching Laurie.

3. Jo liked staying with Aunt March because
   _____ a. she wanted Aunt March's money.
   _____ b. Jo ran away from home.
   _____ c. Aunt March was her mother.
   _____ d. Aunt March had a lot of books and Jo loved to read.

4. This story tells us that, some of the time, even the most loving sisters
   _____ a. are always kind.
   _____ b. do not get along.
   _____ c. would never hurt one another.
   _____ d. really don't love each other.

5. Amy got so angry at Jo one day that she took Jo's writing book and
   _____ a. sold it.
   _____ b. hid it.
   _____ c. put it into the fire.
   _____ d. cut it up.

6. When Jo found out what Amy did with her book, she
   _____ a. kissed her.
   _____ b. hit her.
   _____ c. was very angry.
   _____ d. laughed.

7. Who saved Amy when she fell into the lake?
   _____ a. Laurie
   _____ b. Beth
   _____ c. Meg
   _____ d. John Brooke

8. At the end of this story, Jo is
   _____ a. leaving home for good.
   _____ b. going back to school.
   _____ c. never talking to Laurie again.
   _____ d. sorry for being so angry with Amy.

9. Another name for this story could be
   _____ a. "A Snowy Day."
   _____ b. "Sisters and Friends."
   _____ c. "A Rainy Day."
   _____ d. "Gone Forever."

10. This story is mainly about
    _____ a. cold winter days.
    _____ b. danger near the lake.
    _____ c. sisters sometimes not getting along.
    _____ d. Aunt March.

Check your answers with the key on page 67.

SUNNY DAYS OF SPRING

VOCABULARY CHECK

aunt	fire	job	sisters	write

I. Sentences to Finish

Fill in the blank in each sentence with the correct key word from the box above.

1. We put the _____ out quickly.

2. Please _____ me a letter soon.

3. My _____ is taking me to the party.

4. I have a _____ taking care of a baby.

5. My _____ sleep in the same room with me.

II. Matching

Write the letter of the correct meaning from Column B next to the key word in Column A.

Column A

_____ 1. aunt

_____ 2. fire

_____ 3. job

_____ 4. sisters

_____ 5. write

Column B

a. work for money

b. to put words on paper

c. two girls that have the same mother

d. my mother's sister

e. something burning

Check your answers with the key on page 69.

JO'S SECRET

PREPARATION

Key Words

building	(bil' - ding)	1. the act of one that builds; as birds busy at nest building
		2. any structure such as a house, barn, church, school or factory
		I walked to a big building on the other side of town.
secret	(sē/krət)	1. hidden from the knowledge of others
		2. working in secrecy
		I told my friend the secret hiding place.
story	(stor' ē)	a telling of a happening or a series of happenings
		The teacher told us a story about trains.
their	(thər)	belonging to them
		It was on their way to school, that they lost our books.
time	(tīm)	1. the period during which an action takes place
		2. the period, or point when something happens
		The boys said it was time to go and play.

JO'S SECRET

Necessary Words

fall   ('fól)   the time of year between summer and winter
                                                The trees lose their leaves in the fall.

newspaper   ('nuz pa pər)   sheets of paper printed daily or weekly with the news
                                                The boy put the newspaper in our mailbox.

JO'S SECRET

Jo loves to read and write. Maybe she could do something with her writing.

Preview:
1. Read the name of the story.
2. Look at the picture.
3. Read the sentences under the picture.
4. Read the first two paragraphs of the story.
5. Then answer the following question.

You learned from your preview that Jo wanted to be a

_____ a. writer.

_____ b. dancer.

_____ c. cook.

_____ d. painter.

Turn to the Comprehension Check on page 28 for the right answer.

Now read the story.

Read to find out about Jo's and Laurie's secrets.

JO'S SECRET

One by one, the leaves fell to the ground from their branches. It was now fall.

Jo would go to her room. It was there that she put her thoughts into her writing book. Writing was what she loved to do best. More than anything, Jo wanted to be a writer.

Jo got up one morning. It was time to do something with her writing, she thought. Jo got dressed. She walked to the bus as fast as she could. She was on her way to the city.

When Jo got off the bus, she asked a man where the city newspaper building was. He said it was not far.

When Jo got to the door, she was a little afraid.

"What if they don't like my story?," Jo thought to herself.

Jo went in the building. She talked to a man about her story. He said he would read it. Then he would let her know if he liked it or not.

Coming out of the building, Jo met Laurie. She told him of her secret day in the city. Laurie said he had a secret for her, too. John Brooke was in love with Meg. Jo was not happy about this. She did not want her sister to leave their happy home.

For days, Jo stayed by herself. She did not say anything to Mother or the girls. She did not want them to know that she had been to the newspaper to try to sell one of her stories.

Not too many days went by, when Jo got a letter in the mail. It was from the newspaper. They liked her story. They were going to use it in their newspaper. There was money in the letter, too. Now she could tell her family her secret.

Jo was so happy. After she read the letter, she jumped up and ran to tell Mother and the girls her good news. They were all happy for her. And the money would be a help to them all.

JO'S SECRET

COMPREHENSION CHECK

Choose the best answer.

1. One day, Jo went to the city to
_____ a.   run away.
_____ b.   buy something for Meg.
_____ c.   meet Laurie.
_____ d.   try to sell her story to the
          newspaper.

2. The man at the newspaper told Jo
_____ a.   to go away and never come back.
_____ b.   he would let her know if he liked
          her story.
_____ c.   that her story was not any good.
_____ d.   that he didn't have time to read her
          silly story.

3. Who else did Jo meet in the city?
_____ a.   Laurie
_____ b.   Amy
_____ c.   Mother
_____ d.   Father

4. Laurie also had a secret. He told Jo that
_____ a.   he loved her.
_____ b.   he wanted to run away.
_____ c.   her father was never coming back.
_____ d.   John Brooke was in love with Meg.

5. Jo was not happy about Laurie's secret because
_____ a.   she did not want Meg to ever leave
          their happy home.
_____ b.   she was in love with John Brooke.
_____ c.   she hated John Brooke.
_____ d.   she hated Meg.

6. Jo didn't say anything to Mother and the girls
   about her trip to the city because
_____ a.   she was afraid they would get
          angry.
_____ b.   she always stayed by herself.
_____ c.   she wanted it to be a surprise.
_____ d.   they would laugh at her.

7. At the end of this story, we find out that
_____ a.   the newspaper building burned
          down.
_____ b.   the newspaper didn't like Jo's story.
_____ c.   the newspaper liked Jo's story.
_____ d.   the newspaper sent back Jo's story.

8. Jo wanted to sell her stories because
_____ a.   she had nothing else to do.
_____ b.   she was trying to help her family
          by making money.
_____ c.   her mother told her to.
_____ d.   no one believed in her.

9. Another name for this story could be
_____ a.   "The Surprise."
_____ b.   "Bad News."
_____ c.   "Never to Write Again."
_____ d.   "Meg Leaves Home."

10. This story is mainly about
_____ a.   Laurie following Jo.
_____ b.   John Brooke.
_____ c.   Jo selling one of her stories.
_____ d.   the big city.

Check your answers with the key on page 67.

JO'S SECRET

VOCABULARY CHECK

building	secret	story	their	time

I. Sentences to Finish

Fill in the blank in each sentence with the correct key word from the box above.

1. We tried to keep her party a _____ .

2. I do not know how to tell _____ .

3. They are _____ a new house next door to ours.

4. All _____ things were lost in the fire.

5. We all had to write a _____ about our first day in school.

II. Word Search

All the words from the box above are hidden in the puzzle below. They may be written from left to right or up and down. As you find each word, put a circle around it. One word, that is not a key word, has been done for you.

```
T S E C R E T G
I G W T R B N H
M T Y R S I V A
E A N V D U T I
O Q Z L A R H R
A J I D N U E O
Q U K B Z C I Q
B F O S T O R Y
```

Check your answers with the key on page 70.

This page may be reproduced for classroom use.

MOTHER GETS A LETTER

PREPARATION

Key Words

beautiful	(bū′ tə fel)	1. very pleasing to see or hear *The picture on the wall was very <u>beautiful</u>.*
cry	(krī)	to make a loud cry from pain, fear or joy *The girl started to <u>cry</u> when she heard the bad news.*
long	(long)	not short *I took a <u>long</u> train ride to the city.*
mail	(′māl)	anything such as letters sent from one post office to another *I got lots of <u>mail</u> and cards on my birthday.*
well	(wel)	feel alright in a good way; in good health *After I ate too much food, I did not feel <u>well</u>.*

MOTHER GETS A LETTER

Necessary Words

barber ('bar bər) a person who cuts hair for a living
The man got his hair cut at the <u>barber</u> shop.

MOTHER GETS A LETTER

Mother asks the girls to help her bear the bad news.

Preview: 1. Read the name of the story.
2. Look at the picture.
3. Read the sentence under the picture.
4. Read the first three paragraphs of the story.
5. Then answer the following question.

You learned from your preview that
_____ a. Mrs. March is going out for breakfast.
_____ b. Mr. March is coming home.
_____ c. Mr. March is not well.
_____ d. Mrs. March has a new job.

Turn to the Comprehension Check on page 34 for the right answer.

Now read the story.

Read to find out how Mrs. March gets the money that she needs to
go to Mr. March.

MOTHER GETS A LETTER

Mother called out to the girls. The mail had come. It was a letter from Father.

The girls listened as Mother read to them. She looked like she was going to cry.

"Father is not well," said Mother. "He wants me to go to him."

Mother did not have money to make the long train ride. She would have to go to Aunt March for the money. She did not want to do that.

When Jo heard of this, she ran out of the house in a hurry. She went into town to the barber. He cut off her long, beautiful hair. He gave her money for it.

When Jo got home, she took off her hat. All eyes were on her.

"This money is for you to take the train to go to Father," Jo told Mother. "Now you won't have to go to Aunt March for money."

Mother thanked Jo.

That night Meg was just about to fall asleep, when she heard a cry. It was Jo.

"My beautiful hair," said Jo. "It was the only thing I had that made me look pretty." Meg sat by Jo.

Then they fell fast asleep.

The next morning, the Marches had their breakfast. They were all sad that Mother had to leave them. But they were happy that Mother would be with Father. She could help him get well.

Soon after, a letter came in the mail from Mother. The girls were happy. Father was getting well. They would soon be home.

MOTHER GETS A LETTER

Preview Answer:

c.   Mr. March is not well.

COMPREHENSION CHECK

Choose the best answer.

1. The girls thought their mother was going to cry when
    _____ a. a letter came saying Mr. March **was not well.**
    _____ b. she got a new job.
    _____ c. they told her they were all leaving home.
    _____ d. the dinner was burned.

2. At first, Mother thought she would have to ask Aunt March
    _____ a. to take the girls to the train.
    _____ b. to take her to the train.
    _____ c. for the money to go see Mr. March.
    _____ d. to buy a new hat.

3. Mrs. March did not like to
    _____ a. stay home.
    _____ b. go to work.
    _____ c. cook.
    _____ d. ask anyone for money.

4. When Jo heard that her mother was going to ask her aunt for money, she
    _____ a. went to Laurie's.
    _____ b. went to the barber.
    _____ c. got a job.
    _____ d. got on an airplane.

5. The barber
    _____ a. gave Jo money for her hair.
    _____ b. told Jo to get out.
    _____ c. gave Jo a job.
    _____ d. went to see Mr. March.

6. Jo had her hair cut off because
    _____ a. she didn't want her mother to go away.
    _____ b. she didn't like her long hair.
    _____ c. she didn't want her mother to ask Aunt March for money.
    _____ d. she wanted to look like a boy.

7. Jo cried about her hair when
    _____ a. she looked at her picture.
    _____ b. everyone stopped laughing.
    _____ c. Laurie told her she wasn't pretty anymore.
    _____ d. she thought no one would hear her.

8. Jo cried because she thought her long hair
    _____ a. made her look like her mother.
    _____ b. made her look like a boy.
    _____ c. was the only thing that made her look pretty.
    _____ d. was never going to grow back.

9. Another name for this story could be
    _____ a. "No News."
    _____ b. "Kind Jo."
    _____ c. "Father Comes Home."
    _____ d. "Why Me?"

10. This story is mainly about
    _____ a. how much Jo loves her mother and father.
    _____ b. a girl getting her first haircut.
    _____ c. a long train ride.
    _____ d. a mean barber.

Check your answers with the key on page 67.

This page may be reproduced for classroom use.

MOTHER GETS A LETTER

VOCABULARY CHECK

beautiful	cry	long	mail	well

I. Sentences to Finish

Fill in the blank in each sentence with the correct key word from the box above.

1. I had to wait a _____ time for the bus.

2. That is a _____ ring.

3. I am glad to hear that you are _____ .

4. The baby started to _____ for her bottle.

5. This letter came in the _____ for you.

II. Mixed-up Words

First, unscramble the letters in Column A to spell out the key words. Then, match the key words with the right meaning in Column B by drawing a line.

Column A		Column B	
1. ryc	_____	**a.**	in a pleasing manner
2. lewl	_____	**b.**	a loud call of pain
3. ilam	_____	**c.**	not short
4. utiefulba	_____	**d.**	letters, postcards
5. glon	_____	**e.**	very pleasing to see

Check your answers with the key on page 70.

This page may be reproduced for classroom use.

MEG GETS MARRIED

PREPARATION

Key Words

become   (bi-kəm)   to come or grow to be
The little girl I knew long ago, had become a beautiful young woman.

everyone   (ev′-rē-wen)   every person
Everyone at the party had a good time.

surprise   (sə(r)-priz′)
1. to come upon unexpectedly or suddenly
2. something you don't know about ahead of time
It was such a surprise when my old friend came to see me.

twins   (twins)
1. two persons or animals born at the same time having the same parents
2. two persons or things looking like one another
The twins looked just like their father.

women   (wům iñ′)
1. more than one woman
2. more than one adult female
All the women at the party had on new dresses and hats.

MEG GETS MARRIED

Necessary Words

college	('käl-ij)	1. a place of higher learning 2. higher than high school *I went to <u>college</u> in another state.*
marry	('mar-ē)	to join as husband and wife *The man and woman will <u>marry</u> in church next Sunday.*
own	('ōn)	belonging to oneself or itself *The girl had her <u>own</u> bedroom.*
take	(tāk)	1. to lay hold of 2. to happen *The party was to <u>take</u> place in the back yard.*
wedding	('wed-ing)	a service that takes place when people marry *The <u>wedding</u> took place in a large church.*
will	(wil)	written instructions of what a person wants done with their property after their death *In my <u>will</u>, I leave my ring to my sister Mary.*

People

Daisy and Demi   twins born to Meg and John Brooke

MEG GETS MARRIED

Meg and John were married in the March home. They had a small, but beautiful, wedding.

Preview: 1. Read the name of the story.
2. Look at the picture.
3. Read the sentences under the picture.
4. Read the first two paragraphs of the story.
5. Then answer the following question.

You learned from your preview that
———— a. Jo got married.
———— b. Father is away with the Army.
———— c. Beth is not well.
———— d. no one loves Meg.

Turn to the Comprehension Check on page 40 for the right answer.

Now read the story.

Read to find out what is going on in the March family.

MEG GETS MARRIED

Three years went by. The March girls had become women. Father was home from the Army. He went back to his old job.

Beth had not been well for a long time. The Marches felt Beth could not live too many more years. They watched over her with lots of love.

Aunt March let Amy live with her. It was her wish to make Amy a grand woman. She gave her nice things.

Jo got on with her writing. She was making more money. She would write one story after another. She was now making a name for herself.

Laurie Laurence went away to college. That made his grandfather most happy. Laurie would bring his friends home. The boys would always have eyes for Amy. But Laurie liked Jo the most.

It was no surprise to the Marches when John Brooke asked Meg to marry him. A garden wedding took place at the March home. Friends walked around the grounds. Flowers were all around. There was fine food to eat.

Meg looked grand in her white dress. She got her wish at last. She would now become Mrs. John Brooke.

It was a happy day for everyone but Aunt March. She told Meg she would cut her out of her will. She wanted Meg to marry a man of means. Meg did not care. She was in love and very happy.

A year went by. Meg had twins. She had a boy and a girl. What a surprise to everyone. They were named Demi and Daisy. The March girls loved taking the twins for walks.

The March women were now starting to branch out on their own.

MEG GETS MARRIED

COMPREHENSION CHECK

Choose the best answer.

1. The Marches felt Beth
   _____ a.   was old enough to get a job.
   _____ b.   would not live too many more years.
   _____ c.   wasn't old enough to get married.
   _____ d.   could go live with Aunt March.

2. Aunt March wanted to make Amy
   _____ a.   a little lunch.
   _____ b.   some socks.
   _____ c.   a grand woman.
   _____ d.   go to school.

3. Jo was making a name for herself
   _____ a.   by writing one story after another.
   _____ b.   as a dancer.
   _____ c.   as a teacher.
   _____ d.   as a singer.

4. In this story, we find out that Laurie
   _____ a.   is not well.
   _____ b.   is going to get married.
   _____ c.   doesn't like Jo.
   _____ d.   has gone away to college.

5. Laurie's friends from school like Amy, but Laurie
   _____ a.   likes Jo better.
   _____ b.   hates Amy.
   _____ c.   loves Meg.
   _____ d.   loves Amy.

6. John Brooke asks Meg to marry him. The wedding takes place
   _____ a.   at the Laurence home.
   _____ b.   at Aunt March's home.
   _____ c.   in a big hall.
   _____ d.   at the March home.

7. Aunt March didn't want Meg to marry John Brooke because
   _____ a.   John Brooke was a mean man.
   _____ b.   she wanted Meg to marry someone that had more money.
   _____ c.   she wanted Meg to always take care of her.
   _____ d.   Meg's father didn't like John Brooke.

8. Meg didn't care that Aunt March cut her out of her will because
   _____ a.   John had a lot of money.
   _____ b.   Meg was going to get a good job.
   _____ c.   she loved John very much.
   _____ d.   she had a lot of money herself.

9. Another name for this story could be
   _____ a.   "True Love."
   _____ b.   "A Very Sad Day."
   _____ c.   "Old Aunt March."
   _____ d.   "No Surprises."

10. This story is mainly about
   _____ a.   Mr. March not being well.
   _____ b.   the March girls growing up.
   _____ c.   bad news for John Brooke.
   _____ d.   school days.

Check your answers with the key on page 67.

MEG GETS MARRIED

VOCABULARY CHECK

become	everyone	surprise	twins	women

I. Sentences to Finish

Fill in the blank in each sentence with the correct key word from the box above.

1. Mom was happy that _____ could come to the party.

2. My sister and I are _____ .

3. I wanted to _____ my father with something nice.

4. "What will _____ of me?" cried the lost child.

5. The group of _____ went out to lunch.

II. Crossword Puzzle

Use the words from the box above to fill in the puzzle. The meanings below will help you choose the right words.

Across

1. every body

3. to come upon unexpectedly

5. more than one woman

Down

2. grow to be

4. two persons born at the same time having the same mother and father

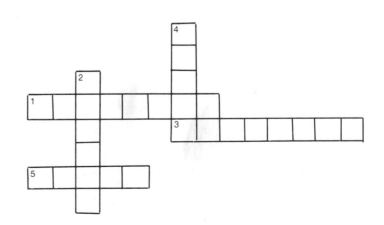

Check your answers with the key on page 70.

This page may be reproduced for classroom use.

JO GOES AWAY

PREPARATION

Key Words

children	(chil′-drən)	1. more than one child; as a boy or girl *The two <u>children</u> got along very well.*
good-by	(gud-bi′)	a farewell word *I had to say <u>good-by</u> to all my friends when we moved to the city.*
great	(grāt)	1. large in size 2. important 3. wonderful; favorite *We had a <u>great</u> time playing in the park.*
met	(met)	past tense of meet *The girls were very happy when they <u>met</u> the boys at the dance.*
school	(skül)	1. a place for teaching and learning 2. to teach; to train *The boys learned much from their <u>school</u> teacher.*

JO GOES AWAY

Necessary Words

family ('fam-ə-le) all of the people that live in the same house; relatives
There are two girls and two boys in my family.

meet (mēt) 1. to come upon or across
2. to go to a place where a person or thing will be
I will meet you in the park near the food stand.

People

Mr. Bhaer a kind teacher Jo meets in New York

Places

New York a large city in the state of New York

JO GOES AWAY

Mr. Bhaer was the children's teacher. He was very kind and loved children.

Preview: 1. Read the name of the story.
2. Look at the picture.
3. Read the sentences under the picture.
4. Read the first two paragraphs of the story.
5. Then answer the following question.

You learned from your preview that

_____ a. Laurie is in love with Jo.
_____ b. Laurie is away at college.
_____ c. Laurie wants to marry Meg.
_____ d. Jo wants to marry Laurie.

Turn to the Comprehension Check on page 46 for the right answer.

Now read the story.

Read to find out about Jo's new job in New York.

JO GOES AWAY

Laurie Laurence came home from college. School was over for him. He could now tell Jo how he felt about her. He had loved her for a long time. He wanted to marry her.

Jo and Laurie met in the park.

"I can't marry you," Jo said to Laurie. "We have had great times and lots of fun. But I love you like a brother."

Laurie was sad and angry. He said good-by to Jo.

Jo thought it would be good to get away. Laurie could forget her if she was not around.

The Marches had friends in New York. They had lots of money. They lived in a big house. They needed help with their two little girls. Jo could help with them in the day. At night, she could write her stories.

The children had a school teacher named Mr. Bhaer. Jo met him her first night in New York. Mr. Bhaer lived in the house, too. He was many years older than Jo. He was not good-looking. But he was kind and loved children. He had very little money.

Jo let Mr. Bhaer read her stories. He liked them. He helped her to write

them better.

As the days went on, Jo liked living in New York. She and Mr. Bhaer would go to the city. They had great times. He showed her new things and places. They went to shows and for long walks.

When spring came, Jo felt it was time to go home. She needed to see her sisters and her mother and father.

Jo said a sad good-by to Mr. Bhaer. She told him to come and see her. She wanted her family to meet him. By now, Jo and Mr. Bhaer had become more than just good friends.

JO GOES AWAY

COMPREHENSION CHECK

Choose the best answer.

1. When Laurie came home from college,
   _____ a.   Grandfather would not talk to him.
   _____ b.   he asked Jo to marry him.
   _____ c.   he married Jo.
   _____ d.   he found his own place to live.

2. Jo told Laurie that
   _____ a.   she hated him.
   _____ b.   she was going to marry John Brooke.
   _____ c.   she loved him like a brother.
   _____ d.   she would marry him.

3. Jo thought it would be best if she went away so that
   _____ a.   Laurie could forget her.
   _____ b.   Grandfather could forget her.
   _____ c.   she could forget Laurie.
   _____ d.   everyone would be happy.

4. Jo went to New York to
   _____ a.   go to school.
   _____ b.   meet Laurie.
   _____ c.   meet her mother and father.
   _____ d.   help friends with their two little girls.

5. When living in New York, Jo met Mr. Bhaer the children's teacher. He was
   _____ a.   the same age as Jo.
   _____ b.   very kind and helped Jo write her stories better.
   _____ c.   a mean, old man.
   _____ d.   not a very good teacher.

6. Jo liked living in New York because
   _____ a.   she liked being away from home.
   _____ b.   she hated her family.
   _____ c.   she liked Mr. Bhaer a lot.
   _____ d.   she liked living in the city.

7. In the spring, Jo went home because
   _____ a.   she missed her family.
   _____ b.   Mr. Bhaer left her.
   _____ c.   the children told her to go away.
   _____ d.   the children were all grown up.

8. Jo told Mr. Bhaer that
   _____ a.   she never wanted to see him again.
   _____ b.   she didn't like the children.
   _____ c.   she was going to marry Laurie.
   _____ d.   she wanted him to meet her famil

9. Another name for this story could be
   _____ a.   "Jo and the Children."
   _____ b.   "Jo Falls In Love."
   _____ c.   "The Mean Old Teacher."
   _____ d.   "Laurie Comes Home."

10. This story is mainly about
   _____ a.   Meg's twins.
   _____ b.   Grandfather Laurence.
   _____ c.   Jo's life in New York.
   _____ d.   Jo writing stories at night.

Check your answers with the key on page 67.

JO GOES AWAY

VOCABULARY CHECK

children	good-by	great	met	school

I. Sentences to Finish

Fill in the blank in each sentence with the correct key word from the box above.

1. I went for a ride in a _____ big airplane.

2. All the _____ laughed at the funny clown.

3. We went over the bridge to _____ .

4. Ann _____ her friend at the park.

5. We said _____ to Dad as the bus pulled away.

II. Mixed-up Words

First, unscramble the letters in Column A to spell out the key words. Then, match the key words with the right meaning in Column B by drawing a line.

Column A	Column B
1. slooch _____	**a.** past tense of meet
2. trage _____	**b.** a farewell word
3. nirchled _____	**c.** a place for learning and teaching
4. yb-odog _____	**d.** more than one child
5. emt _____	**e.** large in size

Check your answers with the key on page 71.

This page may be reproduced for classroom use.

47

AMY AND LAURIE IN EUROPE

PREPARATION

Key Words

another	(ə'nəth-ər)	1. one more 2. an additional one *I would like <u>another</u> chance to win the game.*
right	(rīt)	1. suitable; proper 2. just; upright 3. good *It was <u>right</u> that the children came in from the rain.*
shining	(shī' ning)	1. giving forth light 2. splendid; brilliant *The gold ring was <u>shining</u> brightly in the light.*
talk	('tȯk)	1. to speak 2. words spoken from one person to another *My friend and I had a long <u>talk</u>.*
without	(with aȯt')	1. on the outer side 2. not having; lacking *We cannot get along <u>without</u> our friends.*

AMY AND LAURIE IN EUROPE

Necessary Words

hotel	(hō-'tel)	a place where people can stay and sleep and have meals *We stayed at a big hotel in New York City.*
life	(līf)	the time that a person is alive *My life has been a very happy one.*
nothing	('nə th-ing)	not anything *There is nothing more I can tell you.*

People

Aunt Carroll   an old aunt with lots of money

Places

Europe   a place across the Atlantic Ocean made up of many countries

AMY AND LAURIE IN EUROPE

Amy tells Laurie to try to think of something other than Jo. She wants Laurie to be happy again.

Preview: 1.   Read the name of the story.
2.   Look at the picture.
3.   Read the sentences under the picture.
4.   Read the first two paragraphs of the story.
5.   Then answer the following question.

You learned from your preview that
_____ a.   Laurie was very sad without Jo.
_____ b.   Amy was very sad without Jo.
_____ c.   Laurie went back to school.
_____ d.   Aunt Carroll told Laurie to leave Amy alone.

Turn to the Comprehension Check on page 52 for the right answer.

Now read the story.

Read to find out how Laurie gets over his love for Jo.

AMY AND LAURIE IN EUROPE

Amy was asked by Aunt Carroll to go to Europe with her. Aunt Carroll was a woman of means. Amy was more than happy to go with her. She was used to the finer things in life.

Laurie was sad these days. He was without his Jo. He could picture her shining face. He was not a happy man. He didn't even want to talk. Mr. Laurence thought he could make Laurie forget about Jo. He asked him to go to Europe with him. Laurie had no thoughts one way or the other. He said he would go.

The boat ride to Europe was a long one.

Some time went by. On Christmas Day, Laurie met Amy in his hotel. Her face was shining when she saw him.

Laurie was not going to be in Europe very long. But as the days went by, he and Amy got along very well. They were seeing one another every day.

Sad news came from home. Beth was not doing well. Amy felt it was only right for her to go home. She should see Beth. Laurie said there was nothing she could do at home to help. So she stayed on.

Amy and Laurie went for a walk every day. They talked and laughed. Amy was fun to be with. And she was very beautiful. Laurie could see that he could be happy without Jo. It was right of him to fall in love with another. In time, he did.

Amy and Laurie were married in Europe. The days on the boat going home were happy days for them.

AMY AND LAURIE IN EUROPE

COMPREHENSION CHECK

Preview Answer:

a. Laurie was very sad without Jo.

Choose the best answer.

1. Amy went to Europe with
   _____ a. Jo.
   _____ b. Meg.
   _____ c. Aunt Carroll.
   _____ a. Laurie.

2. Laurie was so sad because
   _____ a. Jo said she wouldn't marry him.
   _____ b. Grandfather would not talk to him.
   _____ c. John Brooke told him to go away.
   _____ d. the March family moved.

3. Mr. Laurence thought he could get Laurie to forget about Jo by
   _____ a. sending him back to school.
   _____ b. taking all her pictures away.
   _____ c. not talking to him.
   _____ d. taking him to Europe.

4. Who did Laurie meet in Europe?
   _____ a. Meg
   _____ b. Amy
   _____ c. Jo
   _____ d. Beth

5. In Europe, Laurie and Amy
   _____ a. had a big fight.
   _____ b. started to see each other a lot.
   _____ c. met Jo.
   _____ d. met Meg and John.

6. The sad news that came from home was that
   _____ a. the March family had moved.
   _____ b. Grandfather's house burned down.
   _____ c. Jo got married.
   _____ d. Beth was not well.

7. As time went by, Laurie and Amy
   _____ a. fell in love.
   _____ b. got tired of each other.
   _____ c. started fighting with each other.
   _____ d. forgot all about home.

8. Before going back home, Laurie and Amy
   _____ a. bought a house.
   _____ b. had a big fight.
   _____ c. told Jo they never wanted to see her again.
   _____ d. got married.

9. Another name for this story could be
   _____ a. "Going Home."
   _____ b. "Christmas Day."
   _____ c. "Good News."
   _____ d. "Happy at Last."

10. This story was mainly about
    _____ a. Aunt Carroll.
    _____ b. Laurie getting over his love for Jo.
    _____ c. all the places Amy saw in Europe.
    _____ d. a very long boat ride.

Check your answers with the key on page 67.

AMY AND LAURIE IN EUROPE

VOCABULARY CHECK

another	right	shining	talk	without

I. Sentences to Finish

Fill in the blank in each sentence with the correct key word from the box above.

1. I am so angry with you that I do not want to _____ to you.

2. I really don't want to go _____ you, so please come with me.

3. That light is _____ in my eyes.

4. She wants to read _____ book about fish.

5. Mother said I did the _____ thing by coming to her.

II. Word Use

Put a check next to YES if the sentence makes sense. Put a check next to NO if the sentence does not make sense.

1. We <u>talk</u> with our ears.　　　　　　　　 _____ Yes _____ No

2. The lion was <u>shining</u>.　　　　　　　　　 _____ Yes _____ No

3. You cannot live <u>without</u> water.　　　　　 _____ Yes _____ No

4. It would not be <u>right</u> for me to take this from you.　　 _____ Yes _____ No

5. Please take <u>another</u> picture of me in my new dress.　 _____ Yes _____ No

Check your answers with the key on page 71.

This page may be reproduced for classroom use.

DARK DAYS FOR JO

PREPARATION

Key Words

anyone	(en' ē-w ən)	1. any person
		2. any body
		I wanted to go to the circus more than anyone.
birthday	(bərth'-dā)	1. the day on which a person is born
		2. the return each year on the date a person was born
		All my friends came to my birthday party.
coming	('kəm-ing)	drawing near; arriving
		My friends were coming to play with me after school.
hard	(hard)	1. not soft
		2. difficult to do
		It was hard for me to do my homework.
sitting	(sit' ing)	1. the act or position of a person who sits
		2. to rest on a chair
		The boy was sitting on a hard chair.

DARK DAYS FOR JO

Necessary Words

knock ('näk)

to make a noise on a door
I ran to the door when I heard the knock.

those (thōs)

plural of that
Those last days of school were hard for me.

umbrella (əm-'brel-ə)

a light, folding frame covered with cloth to protect you from the rain or sun
I took my umbrella to work when it looked like it would rain.

DARK DAYS FOR JO

Beth tells Jo to take care of Mother and Father when she is gone.

Preview:
1. Read the name of the story.
2. Look at the picture.
3. Read the sentence under the picture.
4. Read the first two paragraphs of the story.
5. Then answer the following question.

You learned from your preview that

_____ a. Beth has passed away.

_____ b. Beth has gotten married.

_____ c. Beth went off to school.

_____ d. Beth went off to Europe.

Turn to the Comprehension Check on page 58 for the right answer.

Now read the story.

Read to find out why Jo feels all alone.

DARK DAYS FOR JO

It was spring. Beth was still not well. She looked out her window. She said her last good-by to the birds sitting outside her window. By the next morning, Beth had passed away.

These were dark days for Jo. She missed her sister Beth. She had been with her those last days. It was hard for Jo to fall asleep at night. The days were so long. Jo even found it hard to write her stories.

It was the day before Jo's 25th birthday. She was sitting in her room. She heard two people coming up the walk to the house. It was Amy and Laurie. They had just come back from Europe. How happy they looked. Jo told them how happy she was to see them. She was glad that Laurie was happy again and in love.

The next day the family was sitting in the living room. Jo looked in at them. There sat Meg with her twins. Amy and Laurie looked like a picture of happiness. Jo felt so alone. She did not have anyone for herself, she thought.

Jo heard a soft knock on the door. She ran to open it. There before her was Mr. Bhaer. He had come all the way from New York. He had one of Jo's stories in his hand. A friend of his was going to put it in his newspaper.

Jo wanted her family to meet Mr. Bhaer. He wanted to go for a walk. It was raining very hard. They walked along under his umbrella. Mr. Bhaer told Jo how he felt about her. He loved her more than anyone could. He did not have much money. But he would take good care of her always.

Jo was so happy. At last she had someone she wanted to be with and love. What a happy birthday she was going to have after all!

That year Jo and Mr. Bhaer were married. At last Jo, too, had found happiness.

DARK DAYS FOR JO

COMPREHENSION CHECK

Choose the best answer.

1. In this story we find out that Jo
   _____ a.   cannot sleep.
   _____ b.   is still writing stories.
   _____ c.   has married Laurie.
   _____ d.   misses Beth very much.

2. The day before Jo's birthday, who came to the house?
   _____ a.   Meg and John
   _____ b.   Amy and Laurie
   _____ c.   Grandfather Laurence
   _____ d.   Demi and Daisy

3. Jo was glad that
   _____ a.   everyone was going away.
   _____ b.   she was moving.
   _____ c.   Laurie had fallen in love with her sister.
   _____ d.   her writing days were over.

4. Jo felt all alone because
   _____ a.   she didn't have anyone who loved her.
   _____ b.   everyone was in Europe.
   _____ c.   it was her birthday and she was getting old.
   _____ d.   no one wished her a happy birthday.

5. To Jo's surprise, who came to see her?
   _____ a.   Grandfather Laurence
   _____ b.   Mr. Bhaer
   _____ c.   The two girls she had taken care of
   _____ d.   The newspaper man

6. A friend of Mr. Bhaer's was
   _____ a.   with him.
   _____ b.   getting married.
   _____ c.   going to put one of Jo's stories in the newspaper.
   _____ d.   living next door to Jo.

7. When Jo and Mr. Bhaer went for a walk,
   _____ a.   the sun was shining.
   _____ b.   they took the twins with them.
   _____ c.   Mr. Bhaer asked Jo to marry him
   _____ d.   they went to buy a newspaper.

8. At last Jo, too, had found
   _____ a.   her missing shoe.
   _____ b.   happiness.
   _____ c.   her writing book.
   _____ d.   the umbrella.

9. Another name for this story could be
   _____ a.   "The March Family."
   _____ b.   "Alone at Last."
   _____ c.   "Jo's Love."
   _____ d.   "A Rainy Day."

10. This story is mainly about
    _____ a.   a birthday party.
    _____ b.   a lost umbrella.
    _____ c.   a friend of Mr. Bhaer.
    _____ d.   Jo feeling sad and all alone.

Check your answers with the key on page 67.

DARK DAYS FOR JO

VOCABULARY CHECK

anyone	birthday	coming	hard	sitting

I. Sentences to Finish

Fill in the blank in each sentence with the correct key word from the box above.

1. "Would _____ like to go to the park with me?" asked Mary.

2. Mother was _____ out of the house, when she fell.

3. The little boy will be five years old on his next _____ .

4. Dad was _____ by the door in his new chair.

5. This work is too _____ for me to do alone.

II. Word Search

All the words from the box above are hidden in the puzzle below. They may be written from left to right or up and down. As you find each word, put a circle around it. One word, that is not a key word, has been done for you.

```
H A R D Z F O L
A S U K I J M N
W I A N Y O N E
A T D F E H J K
Y T B G P O Q R
B I R T H D A Y
W N D G K L P R
K G C O M I N G
```

Check your answers with the key on page 71.

This page may be reproduced for classroom use.

LIFE AT PLUMFIELD

PREPARATION

Key Words

grandmother   (grand'-məth-ər)   a father's mother or mother's mother
I went to see my <u>grandmother</u> on her birthday.

important   (im'-pȯrt-ənt)   having great meaning
It is <u>important</u> for everyone to listen to the teacher.

small   (smȯl)   little in size; not very much
All the <u>small</u> boys got to play first.

smart   (smärt)   1. quick to learn
2. bright and amusing
If you want to be <u>smart</u>, you must read books.

such   (sə ch)   so great; so bad; so good, etc.
There was <u>such</u> a loud noise, I jumped up to see what had happened.

LIFE AT PLUMFIELD

Necessary Words

arms   (ärmz)   the parts of a person's body that are between the shoulders and hands

> *My arms are tired from carrying that big box.*

became   (bi kam′)   1. past tense of become
2. came to be; grew to be

> *As the sun went down, it became dark.*

picked   (pikd)   1. past tense of pick
2. chose; selected; took

> *I picked the blue box.*

rest   (′rest)   that which is left over

> *Some of the class went to the park; the rest of the class went to the zoo.*

People

Beth Laurence   is the child born to Amy and Laurie Laurence. She was named after Amy's sister.

Rob and Teddy   the two boys born to Jo and Mr. Bhaer, her husband

Places

Plumfield   the big, old house owned by Aunt March later willed (given) to Jo

LIFE AT PLUMFIELD

Jo wants Plumfield to be a place for boys to grow and learn. They can also help work in the garden.

Preview: 1. Read the name of the story.
2. Look at the picture.
3. Read the sentences under the picture.
4. Read the first two paragraphs of the story.
5. Then answer the following question.

You learned from your preview that Fritz Bhaer and Jo are living

_____ a. with Meg and John.

_____ b. with the Laurences.

_____ c. in Aunt March's old house.

_____ d. in Europe.

Turn to the Comprehension Check on page 64 for the right answer.

Now read the story.

Read to find out what Grandmother March wishes for her "little women."

LIFE AT PLUMFIELD

Aunt March passed away. She left her big old house, Plumfield, to Jo.

Jo and Fritz Bhaer were so happy with their new home. It was their wish to make Plumfield into a school for boys. They worked hard. Plumfield became what Jo wanted it to be. It was a happy, homelike place for boys needing care and kindness. They got their schooling from Mr. Bhaer. That was most important to him.

As the years went by, Jo and Fritz Bhaer had two children. They were boys. Their names were Rob and Teddy. Grandmother March thought them to be smart. They were good-looking, too.

Plumfield had become a place for the March family to meet. They had such good times there. It was a fine fall day for Grandmother March's 60th birthday. It was such an important day. Everyone was there.

Amy and Laurie came. So did Grandfather Laurence. Amy and Laurie had a little girl. They named her Beth. She was a small child, much like her Aunt Beth who had passed away.

Meg and John Brooke had the twins with them. They were older and getting big. They helped with the small children. It was a fun time. The children played with each other. The one who won all the games always thought he was so smart.

The rest of the family picked apples. There were big ones and small ones.

Grandmother March got many nice things for her birthday. Everyone wished her well.

The happy day came to an end. Mrs. March put her arms out. With all her children, and their children around her, she said, "I wish that my 'little women' will be as happy for the rest of their lives as we are today."

LIFE AT PLUMFIELD

COMPREHENSION CHECK

Choose the best answer.

1. Fritz Bhaer thought the most important thing Plumfield could give the boys was
   _____ a.   lots of apples.
   _____ b.   good schooling.
   _____ c.   a place to play.
   _____ d.   a place to swim.

2. As the years went by, Jo and Fritz had
   _____ a.   too much work to do.
   _____ b.   too many apples to pick.
   _____ c.   too many fights.
   _____ d.   two boys of their own named Rob and Teddy.

3. Now all of the March family would meet
   _____ a.   at Plumfield.
   _____ b.   at the Laurence home.
   _____ c.   at Meg's and John's home.
   _____ d.   in Europe.

4. Amy and Laurie Laurence had a baby girl. They named her
   _____ a.   Jo.
   _____ b.   Carroll.
   _____ c.   Meg.
   _____ d.   Beth.

5. In this story we know that many years have passed, because Meg's and John's twins are older and they
   _____ a.   are married.
   _____ b.   are away in school.
   _____ c.   help with the smaller children.
   _____ d.   do all the cooking.

6. Why is everyone at Plumfield in this story?
   _____ a.   It was Grandmother March's birthday.
   _____ b.   It was raining.
   _____ c.   They were helping paint the hous
   _____ d.   They were building a barn.

7. The most important thing to Mrs. March wa that
   _____ a.   she got many things for her birthday.
   _____ b.   Plumfield was a big house.
   _____ c.   her three girls and their families were happy.
   _____ d.   all the children had come to see he

8. Mrs. March wished that her "little women" would always be
   _____ a.   happy.
   _____ b.   more like her.
   _____ c.   better cooks.
   _____ d.   able to move to bigger houses.

9. Another name for this story could be
   _____ a.   "A New School."
   _____ b.   "Hard Work."
   _____ c.   "Who Cares?"
   _____ d.   "A Happy Ending."

10. This story is mainly about
    _____ a.   a big surprise.
    _____ b.   the grown up March girls and the families.
    _____ c.   picking apples.
    _____ d.   a big birthday party.

Check your answers with the key on page 67.

LIFE AT PLUMFIELD

VOCABULARY CHECK

grandmother	important	small	smart	such

I. Sentences to Finish

Fill in the blank in each sentence with the correct key word from the box above.

1. It is not _____ to play with fire.

2. The _____ boy started to cry because he could not find his mother.

3. This is a very _____ day for me.

4. It was _____ a nice surprise to see you.

5. My _____ always brings me surprises.

II. Matching

Write the letter of the correct meaning from Column B next to the key word in Column A.

Column A	Column B
_____ 1. important	a. my mother's mother
_____ 2. such	b. little in size
_____ 3. grandmother	c. quick to learn
_____ 4. small	d. having great meaning
_____ 5. smart	e. so great

Check your answers with the key on page 72.

NOTES

COMPREHENSION CHECK ANSWER KEY
Lessons CTR A-21 to CTR A-30

LESSON NUMBER	QUESTION NUMBER										PAGE NUMBER
	1	2	3	4	5	6	7	8	9	10	
CTR A-21	c	d	a	b	d	a	c	(a)	△d	[a]	10
CTR A-22	a	d	b	c	d	(a)	b	a	△c	[b]	16
CTR A-23	d	a	d	b	c	(c)	a	d	△b	[c]	22
CTR A-24	d	b	a	d	a	(c)	c	b	△a	[c]	28
CTR A-25	a	c	(d)	b	a	c	(d)	c	△b	[a]	34
CTR A-26	b	c	a	d	a	d	(b)	c	△a	[b]	40
CTR A-27	b	c	a	d	b	(c)	a	d	△b	[c]	46
CTR A-28	c	a	d	b	b	d	(a)	d	△d	[b]	52
CTR A-29	d	b	c	a	b	c	(c)	b	△c	[d]	58
CTR A-30	b	d	a	d	c	a	(c)	a	△d	[b]	64

○ = Inference (not said straight out, but you know from what is said)

△ = Another name for the story

▢ = Main idea of the story

NOTES

VOCABULARY CHECK ANSWER KEY
CTR A-21 to CTR A-30

LESSON NUMBER		PAGE NUMBER

21 **CHRISTMAS AT THE MARCH HOUSE**   **11**

I.
1. next
2. hair
3. pretty
4. breakfast
5. money

II.

22 **THE BOY NEXT DOOR**   **17**

I.
1. grandfather
2. party
3. dress
4. window
5. thank

II.
1. Yes
2. Yes
3. No
4. No
5. Yes

23 **SUNNY DAYS OF SPRING**   **23**

I.
1. fire
2. write
3. aunt
4. job
5. sisters

II.
1. d
2. e
3. a
4. c
5. b

VOCABULARY CHECK ANSWER KEY
CTR A-21 to CTR A-30

24 **JO'S SECRET** 29

I. 1. secret
2. time
3. building
4. their
5. story

II.

```
T S E C R E T G
I G W T R B N H
M T Y R S I V A
E A N V D U T I
O Q Z L A R H R
A J I D N U E O
Q U K B Z C I Q
B F O S T O R Y
```

25 **MOTHER GETS A LETTER** 35

I. 1. long
2. beautiful
3. well
4. cry
5. mail

II. 1. cry, b
2. well, a
3. mail, d
4. beautiful, e
5. long, c

26 **MEG GETS MARRIED** 41

I. 1. everyone
2. twins
3. surprise
4. become
5. women

II.

VOCABULARY CHECK ANSWER KEY
CTR A-21 to CTR A-30

27   JO GOES AWAY   47

I. 1. great
    2. children
    3. school
    4. met
    5. good-by

II. 1. school, c
     2. great, e
     3. children, d
     4. good-by, b
     5. met, a

28   AMY AND LAURIE IN EUROPE   53

I. 1. talk
    2. without
    3. shining
    4. another
    5. right

II. 1. No
     2. No
     3. Yes
     4. Yes
     5. Yes

29   DARK DAYS FOR JO   59

I. 1. anyone
    2. coming
    3. birthday
    4. sitting
    5. hard

II.
```
H A R D  Z F O L
A S U K I J M N
W I A N Y O N E
A T D F E H J K
Y T B G P O Q R
B I R T H D A Y
W N D G K L P R
K G C O M I N G
```

LESSON NUMBER		PAGE NUMBER
30	**LIFE AT PLUMFIELD**	65

I.
1. smart
2. small
3. important
4. such
5. grandmother

II.
1. d
2. e
3. a
4. b
5. c